The Scottish Armoury

David H. Caldwell

DAVID H. CALDWELL was educated at Ardrossan Academy, Ayr-shire, and took a degree in archaeology at the University of Edinburgh, graduating in 1973. Since then he has been employed by the National Museum of Antiquities of Scotland, Edinburgh, working on the medieval and more recent collections. His main interests are in weapons and fortifications, and he is doing research on early guns in Scotland. He is a Fellow of the Society of Antiquaries of Scotland.

THE
SCOTTISH
ARMOURY

David H. Caldwell

WILLIAM BLACKWOOD
1979

First published in 1979 by
William Blackwood & Sons Ltd
32 Thistle Street
Edinburgh EH2 1HA
Scotland

ISBN 0 85158 131 5

Printed at the Press of
the Publisher

Contents

Illustrations

Acknowledgement is made to the following for giving permission for copyright material to be reproduced:

(B) Banff Museum
(C) Royal Commission on Ancient Monuments, Scotland
(D) Department of the Environment
(G) Glasgow Art Galleries and Museums
(N) National Museum of Antiquities of Scotland
(R) Royal Scottish Museum

Acknowledgements

I would like to record my debt of gratitude to several friends and colleagues who have given me advice and assistance on arms and armour, in particular Stuart Maxwell of the National Museum, and also Claude Blair, A. V. B. Norman and J. G. Scott. I alone, however, am responsible for the opinions expressed in this book. Finally, I would like to thank my wife Margaret for her encouragement and Tom Gregersen of William Blackwood & Sons Ltd for dealing with a difficult manuscript.

Introduction

THE Scots have a great martial tradition behind them. Not only was there an almost constant need to defend Scotland against aggression from outside, but the country had more than its fair share of internal strife. Small wonder that the Scots were hardy fighters and that distinctive weapons and methods of fighting evolved. Many fighting men left the country to take up mercenary service in Europe and Ireland, and both commanders and other ranks achieved great fame for their steadfastness in battle.

Scotland relied for the most part on fencibles for its defence—the nobles, lairds and yeomen between the ages of sixteen and sixty, who were obliged, when required, to turn out suitably armed for service in the host or national army.

The army of the Solemn League and Covenant, which played a distinguished part under the Earl of Leven campaigning in England in the 1640s, was raised in this manner. After the restoration to the throne of Charles the Second in 1660, Scotland formed its first standing army, but owing to its small numbers traditional levies continued, although at reduced levels. Among the Highlanders the old system remained in use into the eighteenth century, the forces of the Jacobite armies being raised in this way as late as 1746. When a turn-out of men was required, letters were sent to the sheriffs and read at the market crosses of the main towns, and sometimes a fiery cross was carried round the more remote regions. Usually those eligible for military service accompanied their feudal lord or clan chief, and there were laws laid down that a captain should be chosen to lead the men from each parish. There is a delightful account of how one Highlander was called to arms in the 1745 uprising. He had just finished stacking the barley and was on top of the stack when his chief called. He slid down, cast off his long coat, and, taking up his short coat and his gun, went away at once, not to see his wife and children again for several months.

The sheriffs, bailies and other local royal officers were ordered to hold 'wappinschawingis' (weapon-showings) four times a year (later only twice a year) at which the arms and armour of the men under their jurisdiction could be inspected. In the sixteenth century, more and more use was made of *wageours*, or mercenaries, especially for raids against Border thieves. Often armed with hand guns, they were hired also to act as bodyguards, and to hold or besiege castles.

The onus to be well armed lay with the individual, for both his own personal safety and the defence of the country. Up to the fifteenth century a man might also be required to stand trial by battle in legal cases where a verdict could not be arrived at by other means. In 1396 a judicial combat was arranged by Robert the Third between thirty men of Clan Hay, or Kay, and thirty of the Clan Quele, in an attempt to resolve their differences; all but a handful were killed. The Scots' love of fighting was also let loose in tournaments and other martial displays, with less dreadful results. In 1508 James the Fourth held a tournament in honour of Bernard Stewart, Lord of Aubigny, the great French commander of Scottish origin. The lists for this magnificent and colourful affair lay below Edinburgh Castle, in what are now the Princes Street gardens. A Negress at James's court was made the Queen of the tournament.

Many of the weapons used by the Scots were made by Scottish craftsmen, but they were not always able to produce sufficient of high enough quality. Therefore, large quantities of arms and armour were imported from the Continent. The king and governors of the realm built up arsenals to supply the royal household and retainers, and the nobles often saw to the arming of their own retinues. Merchants were encouraged to bring back weapons and materials for making them when their ships went abroad. Finely produced weapons were bought abroad by those who could afford them, but the majority of arms and armour imported were munitions arms, lacking in decoration and often in quality. Scottish craftsmen who were capable of work of a high standard were granted royal titles and fees as a means of encouragement. For example, the positions of Master Armourer, Master Cutler and Master Bowyer were created. To supplement home production, Continental craftsmen were brought over. James the Fourth and James the Fifth particularly encouraged types of Continental craftsmanship hitherto lacking in Scotland. In the sixteenth century royal workshops were set up in Edinburgh Castle and Holyrood Palace for the making of armaments, especially artillery and fine-quality armour. Many of the paid craftsmen manning these workshops were foreigners.

The majority of arms and armour workers were craftsmen who worked in the burghs and belonged to the hammermen incorporations, which grew up in various towns from the late fifteenth century onwards. Hammermen were artisans who worked with metals—goldsmiths, lorimers (who made the metal parts of harnesses), pewterers and bladesmiths. The admission of craftsmen to the hammermen incorporations was strictly controlled. First the prospective craftsman had to serve an apprenticeship, usually of seven years, with a master of his craft; then, to be admitted a freeman, he had to produce a satisfactory 'essay' piece. Some typical examples of the essays for arms and armour makers were those laid down in Edinburgh in the late sixteenth century:

Cutler's essay, 1584: a plain-finished whinger (a dagger or small sword).

Armourer's essay, 1590: a great hit sword (two-handed sword?).

Dagmaker's (gunsmith's) essay, 1594: a hackbut (a long gun) and a dag (a pistol).

On being admitted a freeman, the craftsman could then either work as a journeyman for a master, or become a master himself. If he chose the latter, as many did, he had to acquire his own tools and premises, and usually had to work for a certain period before he was allowed to take on apprentices or other servants. The quality of work of all craftsmen was controlled by the deacons of the hammermen. The various shops were visited regularly, and defective pieces of work had to be destroyed.

Outside the larger towns much of the weapon-making was done by blacksmiths, and in the Highland region some of the craftsmen were probably itinerant.

The Twelfth to the Fourteenth Century

OUR knowledge of warfare and of the weapons used in Scotland prior to the twelfth century is limited. The Norse settlers of the north and west have left us some of their spears and swords in the graves of their leaders, and the Picts, Scots and Britons carved representations of warriors on their stone monuments, often ostensibly meant as figures from the Bible. Some of these warriors are shown mounted on horses and wielding spears, but there is little evidence that warfare was carried on by bands of mounted troops, and certainly not by the heavy mounted troops that were to be such an important element in the early medieval Scottish army.

Scottish kings of the twelfth century, as part of a much wider policy of feudalising their kingdom, took steps to provide for a new fighting force of heavy mounted troops, or knights as they were known. Such troops had shown their worth on numerous occasions elsewhere. The Normans had perfected the art of fighting on horseback and it was through them that the new method of warfare spread to these isles. In the mid-eleventh century, the Scottish king, MacBeth, had made some use of Norman knights, but it was not until the first half of the twelfth century that knights, under David the First, became a significant factor in Scottish warfare. In return for knights' services David and his successors gave grants of lands, at first mostly to foreign incomers. A knight's equipment was expensive and his training long and arduous—hence his status and the grants of lands required to support him.

No weapons or armour of this early period have survived, but they are depicted on contemporary seals. In the first half of the twelfth century a knight's armour consisted of a coat of chain mail, known as a hauberk, reaching to the knees. This had short wide sleeves and a hood to cover the head, and was slit up the back and front for ease in straddling a

5

horse. To complete his battle-dress the knight wore a conical iron helmet with a protective nasal piece. A large triangular-shaped shield, sometimes having a rounded top and a metal boss protruding from the front, was carried on the left arm as additional body protection. Two weapons were used—a spear, gripped firmly between arm and body, and a double-edged sword, more suitable for cutting-strokes than for stabbing. Last but not least in a knight's equipment was his horse, which had to be capable of carrying a considerable weight and of withstanding the shock of battle. The early knights were probably the first in Scotland to use stirrups, which in a charge provided the necessary support for the full weight of man and horse behind the point of a spear.

Our knowledge of twelfth-century Scotland is far from complete, and we can only guess at the number of knights available to the Scottish kings—certainly no more than a few hundred by the end of the century. Many grants of land were made for fractions of a knight's service. In other cases, a mounted man, less completely armed than a knight, may have been provided: for example, a serjeant, or an archer, sometimes mounted. Although the knights were the élite fighting force of the twelfth century, in the main the host fought on foot with spears and axes.

Development of knightly equipment during the twelfth and thirteenth centuries owed more to fashion than to practical design. The sleeves of the chain-mail hauberks were lengthened and drawn in at the wrist, and mail chausses, or leggings, were worn. Surcoats of cloth were worn over the mail, and shields became shorter and squatter. Headgear developed significantly, with pot-shaped iron helmets completely enveloping the head coming into use early in the thirteenth century. At first they were flat-topped and left the neck bare. They were then given rounded tops and flared sides to deflect blows and were made to rest on the shoulders instead of the crown of the head. Such helmets remained in use until the end of the fourteenth century, and as a curious anachronism were depicted on all great seals of Scotland up

*Seal of Walter FitzAlan,
High Steward of Scotland,
c. 1170. A knight on
horseback is armed with
shield and spear to which is
attached a pennon*

*From a twelfth-century seal
found at Raewick,
Shetland. It depicts a
knight on horseback
wearing a hauberk of mail,
and armed with a sword
and a shield with a large boss*

*The Great Seal of Robert
the Second (1371-90)
depicting the King in
contemporary armour, with
great helm, mail sleeves and
chausses, and
heater-shaped shield*

to the end of James the Fifth's reign.

The few extant thirteenth- and fourteenth-century grave effigies lack these helmets, showing only the mail coifs worn underneath; however, a fragment was found at Carluke, Lanarkshire, and a complete helmet with a reinforcing bevor (chin-protector) was found at Castlemilk, Glasgow. Both date to the first half of the fourteenth century. Most swords carved on grave monuments have short quillons (cross-guards), sometimes curving up at the tips, and lobated pommels, a form apparently derived from those on Viking swords. Other pommels are wheel-shaped.

The arms and armour to be worn by the different classes of men were outlined for the first time at Robert the Bruce's parliament held at Scone in 1318. Men worth £10 in goods were to have a sword, spear and gloves of plate and an aketon and a basinet, or a habergeon and an iron hat; and those having goods to the value of a cow were to be armed with a spear or a bow. (The regulations are of particular interest because they indicate precisely the minimum requirements of soldiers of that time.) Aketons were quilted coats worn either by themselves or under armour for added defence, and basinets were simple conical helmets which became more popular than the heavy helmets which completely enveloped the head. Habergeons were mail coats, lighter than the hauberks worn earlier.

Curiously, nothing is said in the Act about war axes, which were undoubtedly used at this time. One or two have survived and are quite similar to those used by the Vikings. Of interest is the famous account in Barbour's poem *The Bruce* of how Robert the Bruce was attacked by the English knight Sir Henry de Bohun prior to the Battle of Bannockburn. In book XII, lines 30-39, we read:

'Schir Henry myssit the nobill kyng;
And he, that in his sterapis stude,
With ax that wes bath hard and gude
With so gret mayn roucht hym ane dynt,
That nouther hat no helme mycht stynt

Grave slab of Bricius MacKinnon at Iona, fourteenth century. The figure is clad in basinet, pisane and aketon. The sword has a lobated pommel

The hevy *dusche* that he him gaf,   [a crushing blow
That he the hed till harnyss claf
The hand-ax-schaft ruschit in twa,
And he doune till the erd can ga
All *flatlyngis*, for hym falzeit mycht.'   [flat

10

The Later Middle Ages

DURING the fifteenth and sixteenth centuries there were notable changes in the types of weapons, and their availability increased to the extent that at Flodden in 1513 the English were moved to remark that the Scots were all well armed. Full plate armour came into use but, generally, the Scots preferred going into battle wearing light armour which was more suitable for the hilly terrain and guerilla-type warfare that they indulged in. By the beginning of the sixteenth century heavily armoured cavalry had entirely disappeared from the battlefields. Many nobles went on raids and to battles on horseback, but dismounted to fight. However, the Lowlands, especially the Borders, did produce lightly armed horsemen. The majority of the host who fought on foot were equipped with spears which were at least 6 eln (18·5 ft) long.

From the fifteenth century onwards the arms and armour of the Highlands showed less development than that of the rest of Scotland. To some extent this was caused by a natural resistance to change, but different traditions of craftsmanship and warfare were equally influential. For example, in the Highlands archers were employed, whereas in the Lowlands they found little favour.

Armour

The evidence for the armour worn in Scotland in the fifteenth and sixteenth centuries comes entirely from funeral monuments and documentary sources.

The gravestone of Gilbert Grenlau at Kinkell in Aberdeenshire (see page 13) depicts the main elements of a noble's armour at the beginning of the fifteenth century. On his head he wears a conical basinet which comes down at the sides to cover his ears. It has two hinges (represented too high up in this case) for a visor, which is not shown but was undoubtedly of the pointed hounskull type then current in Europe. Over his body he wears a habergeon of chain mail, covering his arms and extending to below his hips, on top of which is a breastplate, itself covered by a coat armour which extends to his hips. A mail pisane (collar) protects his shoulders and neck, metal splints his upper arms, and vambraces cover his forearms. On his legs he wears chausses of chain mail, covered with metal splints. Round his hips he wears a stout belt.

Several of the items of this armour remained in common use among the Scottish nobility well into the sixteenth century. Basinets were in service until early in the century in the Lowland region and much later in the Highlands. Often they were reinforced with plate bevors which protected the chin, and plate gorgets covering the neck. Basinets were replaced by sallets—round skulled helmets, often extending into a point at the back to protect the neck, and sometimes provided with bevors and visors. Armets—contoured helmets which enclosed the head—were also used in the early sixteenth century.

By the mid-fifteenth century arms and legs were generally completely encased with defences of plate, and feet and hands were clad in either plate or mail. Short coat armours, often richly embroidered with heraldic devices, were worn until the beginning of the sixteenth century. Some effigies, on the other hand, depict the dead clad in plate with no covering and in these cases beneath the breastplate a fauld of laminated plates of metal can be seen covering the lower part of the torso (see page 14).

Habergeons of mail, or at least padded arming jackets with pieces of mail attached, were probably still worn under the plate armour, to protect especially the upper arms, legs, neck and armpits. At least two effigies show oval- or shield-shaped plates, called besagews, attached at the shoulders as an armpit defence. Pauldrons, fully developed plate shoulder defences covering the neck and shoulders and part of the

Gravestone of Gilbert Grenlau, Kinkell, Aberdeenshire, 1411. He is wearing a conical basinet and a breastplate under his coat armour. His sword is typically Scottish in style

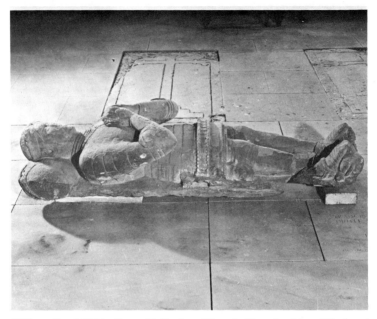

Effigy of c. 1475 in Seton Collegiate Church, East Lothian. The head rests on a great basinet. The lower torso is encased in a fauld of laminated plates over which passes a richly decorated sword belt

breastplate, are shown on an effigy of *c.* 1470 in Corstorphine Parish Church, Edinburgh, but they are exceptional. Similarly, tassets, plate defences for the upper thighs, attached to the fauld, were not common before the sixteenth century.

Much of the armour shown on the grave monuments is undoubtedly the work of Scottish armourers, who were patronised by the kings. Notable among the armourers were several with the name of Moncur—probably all related—one of whom, John Moncur, was working in Dundee in the 1440s and '50s. A John Tait, armourer, possibly of Leith, was feed by James the Fourth in the last quarter of the century, and other Scottish armourers appear in the Lord Treasurer's accounts in the next century. Allan Cochran, an Edinburgh master working in the early 1500s, produced complete stands of armour for the king.

High-quality armour was commissioned abroad by James the Fourth and Fifth, and by the better-off nobles. Attempts were also made to settle foreign armourers, mostly French, in this country with a view to producing fine armour for the royal use. In 1502 a harness (armour) mill was set up in Edinburgh for a French armourer named Passing and his French colleagues, but Passing died soon afterwards. Another harness mill manned by Frenchmen was set up in 1531 at Holyrood Palace, but records do not show how long it remained in operation.

A complete stand of sixteenth-century armour seems to us nowadays to have been a considerable burden on the wearer, weighing as it did somewhere in the region of sixty to 100 pounds. However, the weight of equipment carried by British soldiers during the First World War amounted to nearly sixty pounds, and they were expected to march an average of thirty miles a day. The secret was to have the load well distributed and well secured, and it was essential when wearing armour to be well dressed underneath to prevent chafing.

The process of putting on armour had to be carried out with great care to ensure that each piece was not only securely attached, but fitted comfortably. The procedure was to start at the bottom and work up, overlapping each piece. The help of a servant was essential in this operation. There is an interesting description of William Wallace getting ready for battle in Blind Harry's poem, *The Wallace* (book VIII, lines 1199-1210). Written *c.* 1477-79, the poem describes armour of Blind Harry's time, rather than what Wallace would actually have worn:

'Quhen it was done Wallace can him aray
In his armour, quhilk gudly was and gay
His schenand schoys that burnyst was full *beyn*,   [well
His leg harnes, he *clappyt* on full fast,   [put
A clos *byrny* with mony sekyr *cast*,   [corslet; fastening
Breyst plait, *brasaris*, that worthy was in wer. [arm pieces

15

Besid him furth Iop couth his basnet ber;
His glytterand glowis grawin on athir sid.
He semyt weill in battaill till abid.
His gud gyrdyll and syne his burly *brand*   [sword
A staff off steyll he gryppyt in his hand.'

Fighting men who could not afford plate armour, or who chose to wear something lighter, wore jacks—leather- or canvas-covered padded jackets, reinforced with plates of iron—or brigandines—covered jackets in which the plates were riveted together to give greater strength. Two plates from a brigandine were found at Coldingham Priory in Berwickshire, retaining some of the copper nails which fixed them together and which showed through the textile covering of the jacket forming a decorative pattern. Jacks were sometimes provided with reinforced sleeves or worn with splints. At Pinkie some of the Scots wore brass chains bound round their arms and legs as a defence against cutting, a device also used by Continental mercenaries. A royal enactment of 1481 ordered that men without leg harness were to wear their jacks to the knee, and those with leg harness were to cover the upper part of the harness with their jacks. The form of head protection most commonly in use was the steel bonnet, or knapscull. Sometimes covered in cloth, this head-gear was similar to the simple kettle-hat worn elsewhere at this time, and similar also to the morions worn later in the sixteenth century (see opposite). These were metal caps of semi-oval outline, with flat rims. Many were made in northern Italy and a few have turned up in Scotland.

Complete suits of plate battle armour were used less frequently by the nobility as the sixteenth century went on. At Pinkie in 1547 most were clad in jacks. Plate armour did not, however, disappear from use. It was worn on ceremonial occasions and by mercenary troops. Large quantities of munition armour were imported for the royal retainers. These consisted of halkrig, or corslet—that is, a fore and back plate—a steel bonnet (kettle-hat, or morion) and splints for the arms or legs. In the later sixteenth century,

16

hagbutters—soldiers armed with hand guns—were often equipped with morions and corslets.

A 'Spanish' morion of northern Italian manufacture, late sixteenth century, found at Manton Walls, Ancrum, Roxburghshire. Such helmets were worn by many Scottish fighting men

Highland armour

In the Highlands throughout the fifteenth and sixteenth centuries, and indeed into the seventeenth century, many different types of armour were in use. Grave slabs show warriors wearing padded aketons quilted in long vertical strips and extending to the knees. The quilted sleeves are gathered in at the wrists, and some have reinforcing bands at the elbows. Over the shoulders and covering the neck are broad pisanes of mail; conical basinets without visors, and

17

bevors or gorgets cover the head. A sword belt is invariably worn round the waist. Greaves of plate are worn on the legs of some, and heater-shaped ('shovel-shaped') shields, some of very small size, are carried on the left arm as additional body protection. From documentary sources we learn that the aketons were made of linen and daubed with pitch. In battle, habergeons of mail were often worn over them. A Mackinnon grave monument at Iona dating from the fourteenth century bears one of the earliest representations of this type of armour (see page 9).

Weapons

Spears, axes and bows and arrows, probably in that order of importance, were the main weapons of the later Middle Ages. Although spears were relatively simple and inexpensive to make, many were imported from the Continent, perhaps to help conserve Scotland's dwindling supply of woodland.

Jedburgh staffs

Jedwart (Jedburgh) staffs are first mentioned at the beginning of the sixteenth century and were in common use not only in the Border region, but throughout the Lowlands. In John Major's *History of Greater Britain*, published in 1521, it is stated that the craftsmen of Jedburgh made weapons with blades of steel four feet in length set into oak staffs, and in the burgh records of Edinburgh for 1548, a Jedwart staff is said to be the Scottish term for the French *javelin*—that is, a light horseman's spear. We know from other sources that the staff was capable of dealing a cutting blow as well as a thrust, but it was never described as an axe until a confusion of ideas occurred in the nineteenth century. There are surviving in Scotland a few long-shafted weapons which may be Jedburgh staffs. The pointed, leaf-shaped blades, fixed asym-

18

metrically on the end of the shafts, are exceptionally long—measuring up to four feet—and have a long narrow cutting edge on one side. The staffs are fitted with simple iron vamplates, or stops for the hand, which are normally found only on spears or lances carried by horsemen. Long iron bands extend down the shaft to prevent the head of the staff breaking or being chopped off (see page 21).

Axes

Axes were probably in continuous use as fighting weapons from their introduction by the Vikings in the eighth century. They were used by soldiers fighting on foot, and although the earlier ones seem to have had short shafts, by the fourteenth century many had developed into long-shafted weapons, known variously as gisarmes, battle axes and Danish axes.

Lochaber axes

The west Highland district of Lochaber gave its name to a type of axe which has become famous in Scottish tradition. The earliest reference to such axes occurs in 1501 when it was recorded that James the Fourth bought a 'battle axe of Lochaber fashion'. Twenty years later John Major describes them as being best for cutting and used by 'the wild Scots'. Highland grave slabs and Irish representations of Highland mercenaries—or mercenaries of Scottish descent—show varying forms of axe-heads mounted on long shafts. It is likely that at least some of these are Lochaber axes. The 'Lochaber' may refer only to the length of shaft and not to the shape of the head. In the sixteenth century Lochaber was predominantly a wooded region, and royal workers were sent there to cut timber for gun-carriages and shipbuilding as well as for axe shafts.

By the second half of the seventeenth century Lochaber

axe seems to be the name given exclusively to long-shafted weapons with an axe head, longer than it is broad, with a gently curving cutting edge, and usually with a separate hook projecting from the top of the shaft. In this and the following century it was often used as a ceremonial weapon (see opposite).

Leith axes

In the sixteenth century the axe most commonly in use for warfare in the Lowlands was the Leith axe, which is described as being double-edged and not unlike a halberd, though a little longer and with a hooked blade rather than a spear head. Halberds were imported from the Continent in large quantities from the beginning of the sixteenth century and, like Lochaber axes, were often used as ceremonial weapons.

Swords

In the Middle Ages, as in earlier centuries, the sword was the most prestigious, and the most costly, weapon. We do not know how many people could afford them, but it seems unlikely that many of lower standing than nobles and lairds, or their close associates, would have carried them before the sixteenth or seventeenth centuries. By the beginning of the sixteenth century the sword had developed into several forms for different uses.

Several swords from the late fourteenth century to the early sixteenth—mostly associated with the Highlands—have survived, and others are depicted on west Highland grave monuments. Some of the single-handed varieties are considerably longer in the blade than earlier types. Most have quillons which point upwards—that is, towards the tip of the sword—and end in lobe-shaped or spatulate terminals. Projecting from the hilt on each side of the blade are tongues

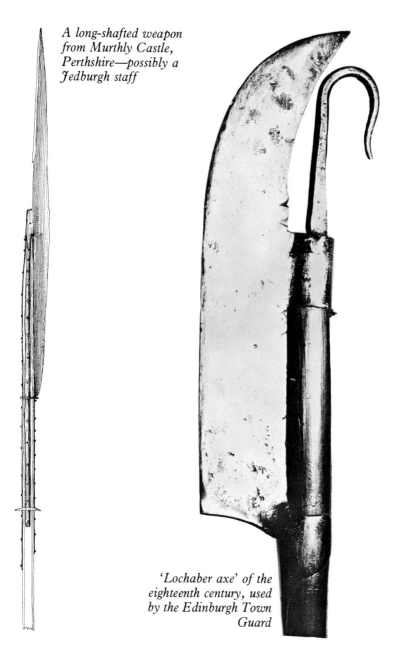

*A long-shafted weapon
from Murthly Castle,
Perthshire—possibly a
Jedburgh staff*

*'Lochaber axe' of the
eighteenth century, used
by the Edinburgh Town
Guard*

21

of metal, or langets, acting as strengthening devices. The pommels are either of the earlier segmented variety, wheel-shaped or, later, globular, with the tang of the hilt projecting up through the top. In the later swords the hilts are often much longer and were obviously designed to be used with two hands if necessary. An early surviving example in the National Museum of Antiquities has a wheel-shaped pommel, quillons swelling slightly towards their tips, and very short langets (see below). Its grip measures slightly less than four inches—not long enough for two hands. It can perhaps be dated to about 1400, although a similar sword is shown on the seal of King John (Baliol) of *c*. 1292. A more fully developed sword of this type, which has a much longer grip, can be seen in Glasgow Art Gallery and Museum.

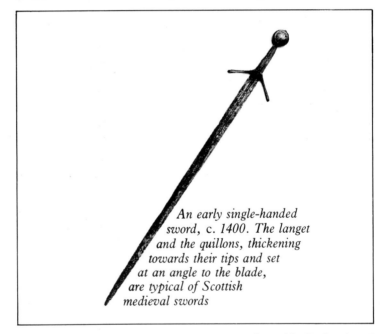

An early single-handed sword, c. 1400. The langet and the quillons, thickening towards their tips and set at an angle to the blade, are typical of Scottish medieval swords

A number of these swords have been found in Ireland and were presumably taken there in the fifteenth and sixteenth centuries by the mercenaries coming from the Highlands and

Islands. Similar swords may also have been used in the Lowlands, but unfortunately we do not have such a fine series of grave slabs as those in the west Highlands to confirm this theory. Certainly a few fifteenth-century slabs in the east depict them, such as the slab of Gilbert Grenlau at Kinkell, Aberdeenshire (see page 13).

By the early sixteenth century the names of several different types of swords were recorded in documents. Halflang swords were similar to those just described, and had enough room on the grip for two hands. Arming swords had shorter blades and were for use with one hand. Less an encumbrance than the longer swords, they were often worn every day.

At that time it was fashionable to wear swords with civilian clothes. Many of these were little more than long daggers, like the baslars (English: baselards) worn at the beginning of the century. Whingers (English: hangers) replaced baslars in popularity and are often described as being daggers. James the Fourth had a curved baslar of the Turkish fashion, and many whingers had similarly shaped blades. The small curved swords depicted on contemporary wood carvings and paintings are probably whingers. Rapiers, most likely imported from the Continent for the nobility, are recorded from the beginning of the sixteenth century. They were used for duelling, together with parrying daggers held in the other hand. Portraits of the second half of the century show noblemen with rapiers and daggers *en suite*. Since mail or plate gloves were no longer worn, both rapiers and daggers had knuckle guards and parrying rings to give protection to the hand. Yet other swords were for use with bucklers, small circular shields used when fighting on foot. Two of these measuring about a foot in diameter are depicted on grave slabs at Keills and Iona. Tooks, long, pointed, stiff-bladed swords designed to penetrate the spaces in plate armour, were used for fighting on horseback. An English account of the Battle of Pinkie in 1547 describes the Scots as being armed with swords 'all notably brode and thin, of excedinge good temper and vniuersally so made to slyce, that as I neuer sawe none so good, so think I it harde to deuyse ye better'.

The blades, then as later, were undoubtedly imported from the Continent. Unfortunately, we do not know what type of hilts they had.

Two-handed swords

In the fourteenth and fifteenth centuries swords of immense size were being made in Europe, but it was not till the sixteenth century that exclusively two-handed swords came into common use. These were weapons of prestige, borne by captains of mercenary bands, or by well-tried soldiers entrusted with special duties, such as guarding the standard. So popular were they in Scotland that their use was encouraged by the government as early as 1513, after the great disaster at Flodden, and continued into the early seventeenth century.

Quite a number have survived, possibly because their great size attracted the curiosity or admiration of later generations, or because they were used for ceremonial purposes. Some are said to have been used by Wallace or Bruce, or their contemporaries, but in all cases such views are erroneous. The hilts often exceed twenty inches and the blades vary from three and a half to four and a half feet and have rounded tips since they were used primarily for cutting. They are generally of German manufacture. In the earlier examples the hilts often have simple bar quillons, but side rings, one to each side of the hilt, are more characteristic. The quillons are in the form of bars turned up abruptly at the ends and ending in knobs; there are short langets over the top of the blade. Pommels are typically globular in shape, but there are also lemon- and pear-shaped types (see opposite). Sometimes the side rings are filled in with decorative plates of metal.

Another type of hilt found on two-handed swords from the late sixteenth century consists of two shell-shaped guards covering the lower part of the hilt, and broad quillons, sometimes counter-curved (see opposite). The essay piece of Robert Lyal, a guardmaker admitted by the Edinburgh hammermen in 1583, was 'a pair of clam skellit gairds' (that is, *one* guard) and a 'pair ribbit gairds'.

24

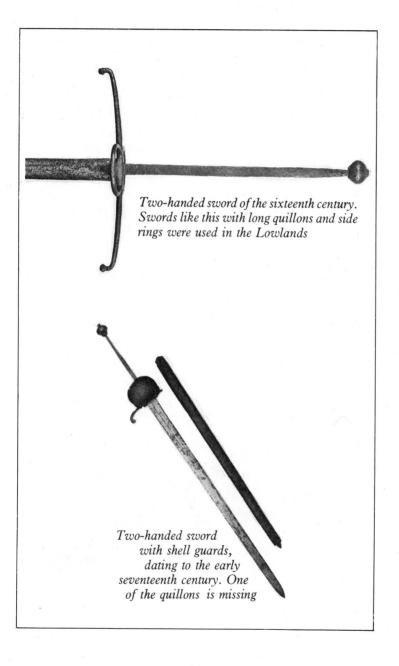

*Two-handed sword of the sixteenth century.
Swords like this with long quillons and side
rings were used in the Lowlands*

*Two-handed sword
with shell guards,
dating to the early
seventeenth century. One
of the quillons is missing*

Claymores

In the Highlands two-handed swords also were in vogue in the sixteenth century but took a different form from those described above. The name given to them is claymores (*claidheamhmór* in Gaelic, meaning great sword). One which is carved on a grave slab at Kirkapoll on Tiree, dateable to 1495, is the earliest evidence of their existence. They apparently developed out of the smaller Highland swords.

On most surviving examples the quillons point up towards the end of the blade, though many shown on grave monuments are placed horizontally. They taper from hilt to tip, resembling a diamond shape in cross-section, and terminate in quatrefoils made up of hollow rings of metal. Long tapering langets are invariably provided, and in the earlier examples the wheel-shaped pommels are relatively small in size (see below). In later examples the pommels are large and globular like those on early basket-hilted swords. Claymores are somewhat smaller than the Lowland varieties of two-handers, and, as with those, remained in use into the seventeenth century.

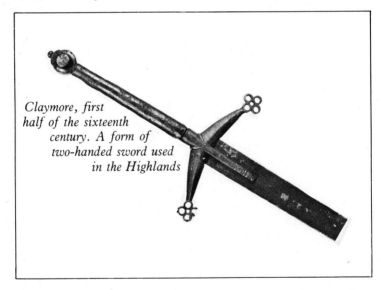

Claymore, first half of the sixteenth century. A form of two-handed sword used in the Highlands

Daggers

Knives have served for a variety of purposes in all ages, but in their specialised form as daggers they emerged in Scotland only in the fourteenth century. The first evidence of them in documents and on grave effigies dates to the later part of the century. Two very fine bronze dagger pommels of the fourteenth century, in the National Museum of Antiquities in Edinburgh, were probably mounted on daggers of good quality. One is circular with a frilly edge, and is decorated with a coat of arms and other devices. The other is crescent-shaped, originally inlaid with enamel work, and was found at Fortingall in Perthshire. It is of French workmanship (possibly from Limoges) from the late fourteenth century. One or two small daggers from the fifteenth century have survived and are fitted with short quillons and double-edged, pointed blades. Many examples of fine daggers are shown on effigies.

In the sixteenth century, daggers with single-edged blades and hilts with ballocks were worn with civilian clothing. These were variants of a type common in Europe. An early ballock dagger found at Coldingham Priory has the bottom part of the ballocks formed of iron and a small by-knife with it (see over). Such a dagger is depicted on a statuette on Stirling Castle Palace. The statuette dates from the early 1540s and is said to represent James the Fifth. A similar dagger was found buried with a body at East Langton, Midlothian. The earliest representation is in fact on the grave slab of John Drummond at Inchmahome Priory in the Lake of Menteith, dateable to the late fourteenth century.

Bows and arrows

Archery never achieved the importance in Scotland that it did in England, though it was by no means neglected. In the fifteenth century a determined attempt was made by James the First and James the Second to improve the quality of

Quillon dagger found near the stone of Clochmuat, Badenyon, Aberdeen. Late fourteenth or fifteenth century

Ballock knife from Coldingham Priory, Berwickshire, c. 1500. The lower part of the ballocks are of iron and along the backed blade is the wooden hilt of a small knife originally fixed in a pocket of the sheath

28

archery. The playing on Sundays of football and golf was banned so that everybody could practise archery at butts— long levelled pieces of ground—beside parish churches. The butts at Linlithgow Palace may date from about this time. Despite such royal decrees, most Lowlanders engaged in archery probably mainly as a hobby or for shooting birds and game. The situation was rather different among the Highlanders, who were still using bows in battle in the second half of the seventeenth century. The Earl of Argyll supplied a contingent of Highland archers for the Battle of Pinkie. There were numerous bowyers working in Scotland, supplying not only bow staves and arrows but spear shafts as well. It is interesting, however, that English bows were greatly valued and that an English bowyer was allowed, and indeed encouraged, to set up business in Edinburgh in the first half of the sixteenth century. In 1676 the Royal Company of Archers was formed—or reconstituted—to encourage the noble art of archery. It is now the Royal Bodyguard for Scotland.

Crossbows, used mostly for siege-work and hunting, were of great importance from an early date. There were royal crossbow-makers in the sixteenth century, including a Frenchman, John Tesart. James the Fourth was keen on crossbow hunting and several payments were made by the Lord Treasurer in connection with James's crossbows. Because crossbows were far too stiff to be spanned by hand, windlasses had to be used. These instruments worked on the block-and-pulley system. Another type of spanning instrument, the cranequin, worked on the rack-and-pinion principle, and was more popular than the windlass because it could be operated by a hunter on horseback. At Stirling Castle Palace there is a fine statue, dating from c. 1540, of a man spanning a crossbow with a cranequin. The bow is held firmly with the left hand and one foot is placed in a stirrup attachment fixed to the end of the stock, while the handle of the cranequin is turned with the right hand (see over).

Another type of bow that made its appearance in the fifteenth century was the pellet bow, used for hunting birds

Sculpture of a man spanning a crossbow, Stirling Castle Palace, c. 1540. Note how the bow is held with one foot in a stirrup attachment while the string is pulled taut by winding a cranequin

and small game. It fired stones or small clay pellets. Crossbows were also adapted to fire such projectiles.

Artillery

The invention of guns was the most significant development in the field of weapons since the first use of metals, and the Scots did not lag far behind the rest of Europe in their use. By 1380 certainly, and probably much earlier, guns had arrived in Scotland in the form of primitive wrought-iron cannon of small size. James the First and James the Second acquired much larger guns, or bombards, notably the famous Mons Meg which can be seen at Edinburgh Castle. Mons Meg was long thought to have been made by a blacksmith in the south-west of Scotland for use at the siege of Threave Castle, Kirkcudbrightshire, in 1456, but as might be guessed from the name, it was made at Mons in Belgium in 1449 and brought to Scotland as a gift from the Duke of Burgundy in 1457. In the 1450s James the Second used his bombards to suppress the Black Douglases in a series of sieges of Douglas strongholds. In 1460, at the siege of Roxburgh Castle, he was killed when one of his own guns broke on firing, and he thereby achieved the unenviable distinction of being the first sovereign, of any country, to be killed by gunfire.

Smaller wrought-iron guns—often called serpentines—mostly breech-loading, were probably being manufactured in Scotland at this time. It was technically easier to make these open-ended at the breech and to plug in a separate container with the powder, or powder and shot, when firing. They must have been rather inefficient and often as dangerous to the gunner as to the foe.

In 1473 there was a further step forward with the founding of bronze pieces of artillery. Cast bronze guns were more efficient than their wrought-iron brethren, since they fired iron or lead shot rather than the stone balls normally used in wrought-iron guns. Packing a much more powerful punch, they were at the same time considerably lighter, and were invariably pivoted on trunnions which made for better and lighter mounting. Some of the early founding was done in Stirling, but in 1511 a foundry was established in Edinburgh Castle. From the beginning it was under the charge of a Scotsman, Robert Borthwick, though he had several foreigners working under him. Borthwick was no doubt responsible for making some of the guns known as the 'Seven Sisters' that were used by the Scots at Flodden and which greatly impressed the English. The whole idea of the Seven Sisters so appealed to the Scots that in time the title was transferred to the guns on the Half-Moon Battery at Edinburgh Castle. In 1716, they were carted off to London to be melted for scrap, and we are told that it 'was like to break all the old women's hearts in town'. After Flodden, Borthwick and his successors continued to make guns for the royal use, and the foundry was still in operation in 1558.

Many of the nobles also supplied themselves with artillery for the defence of their houses. These were small pieces suitable for firing from wall-tops or gun-loops. A number of these guns, however, must have come from abroad.

Hand guns

Hand firearms made their appearance in Scotland at the end of the fifteenth century and were given the name culverins. James the Fourth took great delight in them and made a habit of staging shooting matches with his courtiers. From time to time his Lord Treasurer made payments to the people who outpointed the king. But since there are no records of what, if anything, his opponents paid him, he has the misfortune to be remembered as a loser. His son James the Fifth also took an interest in shooting, but the fact that the Lord Treasurer had to pay compensation to a Stirling woman for a cow that the king had shot suggests that he had a lot to learn.

In the course of the sixteenth century, hand firearms became more common, many mercenaries being armed with them. Large quantities of guns were imported. The earliest surviving Scottish examples date from the last two decades of the century—a small group of richly decorated barrels, lacking their locks and stocks. They are engraved and inlaid with copper and silver in a style which was to become characteristic of all fine Scottish firearms. Presumably fitted with simple match-locks, the guns were fired by the lowering of an arm with a lighted match into the powder pan.

The Flowering of Scottish Craftsmanship

BY the end of the sixteenth century several Scottish arms and armour makers were manufacturing not only competent weapons, but pieces of great artistic merit. There was a great flowering of craftsmanship at the beginning of the seventeenth century, especially in the east coast towns, where Dundee took a lead in the production of pistols. The decorations used—strapwork, acanthus, foliage and flowers— owed their inspiration to the classical designs regenerated in the great Renaissance of European art in the sixteenth century. From as early as 1540, these influences were transmitted to craftsmen working in stone, wood and metal, as well as to the makers of weapons. However, the best work in weapons was done in the first quarter of the seventeenth century. The apparent falling away of craftsmanship during the middle of the century was perhaps caused by the Civil Wars and Cromwell's invasion of Scotland.

Less and less armour was worn as the century progressed. During the Cromwellian period great buff coats, pot helmets and heavy breastplates, proof against bullets, were worn by many of the troops, horsemen often being more heavily armed; but jacks also remained in use. The main weapon was the broadsword, usually fitted with a basket hilt, whereas daggers, small swords and whingers were worn with civilian dress. Firearms were now in common use, and, as we shall see, Scotland had a distinctive contribution to make in this field. As in previous centuries, though, large quantities of munitions were imported from the Continent, especially sword blades, gun barrels and other parts, and munition armour.

The seventeenth century saw an even greater divergence between the Lowlands and the Highlands in methods of warfare. In the Highlands, where speed and mobility were vital factors, broadswords and targes (shields) proved an effective combination. Long-shafted weapons were almost, if not entirely, done away with, and success in battle depended on surprise and the prowess of individuals. Among the Lowlanders, long-shafted weapons remained in favour, though they were largely being replaced by firearms, and emphasis was placed on well-drilled companies and regiments of men acting in concert.

It was a time of much bloodshed. In 1666 and 1679 Covenanters from the south-west rose in rebellion and despite government attempts to disarm potential rebels, most of Scotland remained armed until the end of the century. The standing army was never of a great size and there was still a commitment on the people to do service in the militia. In 1669 it was reckoned that throughout Scotland 10,000 militiamen could be raised. In the south, Covenanters attended conventicles on the moors, armed with swords and guns—and even as late as the early eighteenth century it was said to be normal for Highland gentlemen's servants to carry guns on all occasions, even to church.

During this violent period men such as the Earl of Leven and David Leslie emerged as great military leaders. Many a Scot received a good military training in the Continental wars. There was a wide interest in military matters in the country, extending even to the poet, William Drummond of Hawthornden, who in 1627 took out a patent for developing military machines. A notable military device of the period, for which the Scots can take some credit, is the invention of leather guns—light field pieces of iron or bronze bound with leather. They were used by the Swedish king Gustavus Adolphus in the late 1620s. Two Scotsmen, Robert Scott and James Wemyss, claimed to be among the first to develop these and examples are preserved in the Museum of Antiquities in Edinburgh.

Dudgeon daggers

An interesting group of daggers from the beginning of the seventeenth century are the dudgeon daggers, which are descendants of the earlier ballock knives. They are long and slender in appearance with stiff blades of a diamond-shaped cross-section, and often with flat panels on them. Typically, the hilts are of boxwood, heather root or ebony, with emaciated ballocks and faceted grips swelling towards the top (see below). The blades are etched and gilded with panels containing foliage designs, coats-of-arms and inscriptions, usually couthy Scots comments such as 'God gyde the hand that I instand' and 'Ask me not for schame, drink lis and by ane'. A few show dates ranging from 1605 to 1624, and many bear makers' marks on the blade, often in the form of a crowned letter inlaid with copper. Unfortunately, it has not yet been possible to identify with certainty any of the makers.

Many of these daggers are to be found in collections outside Scotland, indicating that their popularity spread over the Border at an early date. Sword blades also were etched

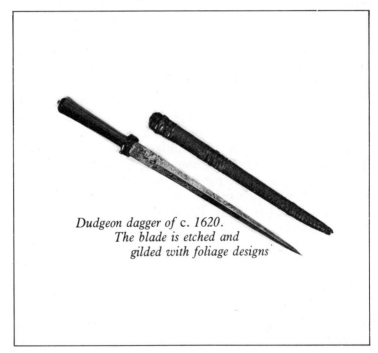

Dudgeon dagger of c. 1620.
The blade is etched and
gilded with foliage designs

and gilded at this time. Among the few which have survived are some on which coats-of-arms and dates obviously belonging to much earlier times were engraved on the blades.

Early basket-hilted swords

The characteristic fighting swords used by the Scots in the seventeenth and eighteenth centuries were fitted with a basket hilt. Such swords were worn also with civilian clothing, as noted in a scurrilous seventeenth-century English poem about the Scots flooding to London in the wake of James the Sixth:

'The sword at thy back was a great black blade,
With a great basket hilt of iron made,
But now a long rapier doth hang at thy side,
And huffingly doth this bonny Scot ride.'

Many of the blades were broad, that is, double-edged, though in the eighteenth century backed blades, lighter and single-edged, were much used. The blades were mostly the work of Continental swordsmiths, especially from the German town of Solingen, and many bear the name of Andrea Ferrara (in various spellings). There was a north Italian swordsmith of this name in the late sixteenth century but, in all cases, his name on Scottish swords is a forgery. It seems 'Andrea Ferrara' was used by the German smiths as a mark of quality when selling blades to the Scots, who became particularly attached to the name. Other selling gimmicks took the form of slogans cut into the blade, like 'Gott bewahr die oprecte Schotten'—God protect the honest Scots.

Basket-hilted swords were designed mainly for cutting, and the Highlanders used them in combination with targes. The origins of the basket type of hilt are not clear. In western Europe, from the sixteenth century, several swords were developed with a protective framework of metal plates and bands enclosing the hand. As far as Scotland is concerned, for an ancestor of the basket-hilted sword we must look back to the buckler swords in use from the beginning of the sixteenth century. As the name suggests, these were used together with small circular shields known as bucklers, and were carried by lightly armed men on foot. Buckler swords must therefore have been used in a similar way to the basket-hilted swords of later times.

Fighting lightly armed with a slashing-sword and shield was already well established among the Scots by the time of the Battle of Pinkie in 1547, though whether or not their swords were mounted with basket hilts we do not know. Certainly by the end of the century the English associated the Scots, or at least the Highlanders, with basket-hilted swords, to such an extent that they were often called Irish hilts, the Highlanders being called Irish by the English. Highland hilts and 'ribbit gairdis' are two further descriptions which probably were applied to the basket-hilt, and such hilts were being manufactured in the Lowland burghs as early as 1583.

Some basket-hilted broadswords dateable to the sixteenth century survive, but it is not always clear whether they are of Scottish or English make. The main characteristics of all basket hilts is the globular-shaped framework enclosing the hilt, which is made up of vertical bars or bands with panels between them (see opposite).

Many of the earliest basket hilts that were probably of Scottish workmanship are made up of flat steel strips and riveted together or cut out of sheet metal. They are often referred to as ribbon hilts. Some of the earliest have projecting quillons, but by the beginning of the seventeenth century, these had been reduced to a single slight 'snout' at the front. Early pommels tend also to be globular, but conical ones are the most common form on seventeenth-century and later basket hilts. S-shaped strips and cross-and-circle panels were used to fill in the spaces between the vertical bars, and these motifs are also typical of many later swords. The few swords of this period which have survived in good condition are often japanned and gilded, with shagreen-covered grips and leather linings to the hilt.

Basket-hilted broadsword with long counter-curved quillons, late sixteenth century

Ribbon-basket hilts were still being produced in the late seventeenth century, but in the second half of the century emphasis shifted to other types, basically similar in design but made up of bars of metal rather than strips. They are often decorated in a rudimentary fashion with incised lines and ring-and-dot motifs, and they have two looped bars below the hilt acting as a parrying device (see opposite).

In the Lowlands swords with other types of hilts were more commonly in use in the seventeenth century, but few have survived. Mortuary hilts were cast and engraved with decorations including heads said to represent the dead King Charles the First. Other swords with hilts probably of Scottish manufacture are preserved in the Museum of Antiquities and the Glasgow Art Gallery and Museum. One of the main types has two side rings filled in with pierced metal plates and knuckle-bows with counter-guards. A fine silver-hilted sword of this type, exhibited in the Museum of Antiquities, was made by the Edinburgh goldsmith Henry Beathune at the beginning of the eighteenth century. The swords were often used by mounted troops, and those which survive are traditionally associated with the Covenanters.

A few whingers or hunting swords of the seventeenth and early eighteenth century have been recognised as being of Scottish workmanship. These short swords, mostly with curved blades, are the successors of the whingers worn in the sixteenth century. The hilts are quite simple with bone or horn grips and brass knuckle-guards, and pommels. Usually they have one side ring or shell. It is known that there was a well-established cutlery industry in the small Ayrshire town of Kilmaurs in the later eighteenth century, and a particularly fine hanger with silver hilt and inlaid tortoise-shell grip, with marks thought to be those of David Bigart of Kilmaurs, is preserved in the Glasgow Museum. Such small swords were used also in the Highlands. The Museum of Antiquities possesses an example complete with a sheath and a pocket for a small knife; its grip is carved with interlace similar to that found on early eighteenth-century dirks.

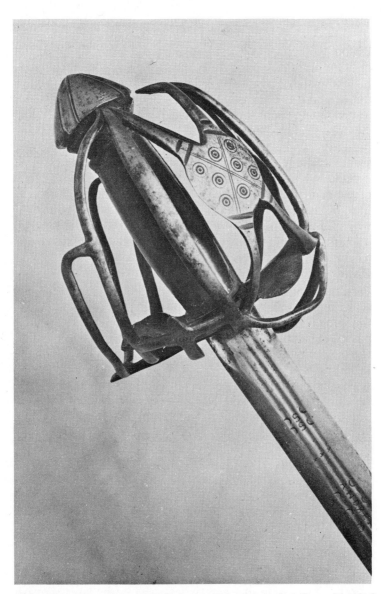

Basket-hilted broadsword with ring-and-dot decoration. Second half of seventeenth century

Pistols were certainly used in Scotland prior to 1550, but only by those rich enough to afford them. Most of the early pistols which have survived are richly decorated luxury items, and it is clear that when the Scots turned their hands to producing them they made weapons of prestige excelling all others. The beginnings of the Scottish pistol-making industry can be traced back to the second half of the sixteenth century and to the craftsmen in the larger burghs, especially Dundee, Edinburgh and Canongate. By the turn of the century there were several specialised craftsmen calling themselves gunmakers or dagmakers—dag being the word for a specific type of pistol. The earliest of these dagmakers known to us by name is David Clerk, who was working in Edinburgh in 1578.

Pistols were certainly used in Scotland prior to 1550, but the numerous Acts of Parliament aimed at preventing the practice by those who came to court or were in proximity to the king. The Privy Council and Parliament incessantly passed legislation banning the wearing of guns, while noting the ineffectiveness of similar legislation already passed on the same subject.

By the beginning of the seventeenth century, two main types of Scottish pistols had emerged—those with fishtail butts and those with lemon-shaped butts (see page 44). They are also distinguishable by being stocked in either wood or metal, the latter being the commonest of those that survive. Exhibited in the Dresden Historical Museum, the oldest surviving pair of wood-stocked pistols, dated 1598, have typical reinforcing metal mounts. In Scotland, however, pistols stocked entirely in metal are much more characteristic of the early seventeenth century and later. The Scottish craftsmen's predilection for metal may be explained by the fact that they came from metal-working backgrounds and worked within the hammermen incorporations of the burghs. Two other characteristics—shared by later Scottish pistols—which might be noted for these early seventeenth-century pistols are the lack of trigger guards and the addition of belt hooks.

Fishtail-butted pistols were usually made of brass, whereas lemon-butted pistols were made of brass and steel. Similar types of butts were used on Continental pistols and it was probably from the Low Countries and France that the designs came to Scotland, though their forms are not identical. Some of the lemon-butted pistols are of great length, and some even have extending butts so that they could be fired from the shoulder. The decoration, which is distinctive, consists mainly of engraved flowers, foliage and strapwork, in a style typical of Lowland Scotland.

The early pistols are operated by snaphance locks (see page 44). To fire the pistol, the cock is forced back against a powerful spring until it is held in place by a small lug projecting through the lock plate. By putting pressure on the trigger, the lug is retracted, causing the cock to be released. A piece of flint held securely in the jaws of the cock is snapped with great force on to a 'steel' positioned above the powder pan, causing a spark which ignites the powder. The powder in the pan in turn ignites the main charge in the barrel. An additional feature on all the locks is a pan-cover to keep the priming powder dry and to prevent it from blowing away. The cover is pushed forward by a small lever as the cock is released. Once loaded and cocked, the pistol can be made temporarily safe by moving the steel out of the cock's path.

Snaphance locks are first mentioned in Sweden about 1550 and a little later in Germany. In Scotland the term 'snap-work' was used to describe locks which we think were of the snaphance type as early as 1568, which is earlier than the known use of these locks in England and Holland, although it has been claimed that the Scottish snaphance was derived from one of these two countries. By the beginning of the seventeenth century on the Continent, snaphances were considered to be a Scottish development.

It is certain that these early Scottish pistols were very much prized, and they are found in the major arms col-

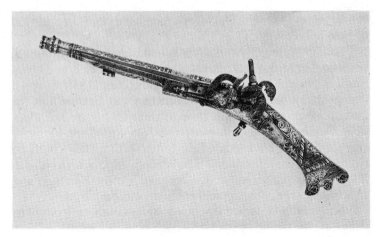

*One of a pair of brass fishtail pistols with snaphance locks signed I L
(James Low of Dundee?), 1611. They belonged to Louis the Thirteenth
of France and bear his arms*

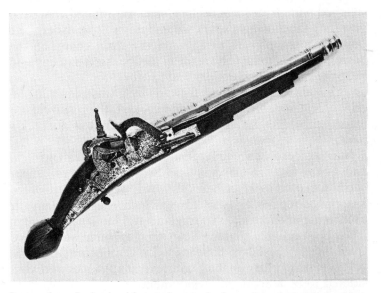

*Lemon-butted pistol with wooden stock, brass barrel and lock plate,
signed R M (Robert Mosman of Canongate?) 1625*

lections of the world. Some may have been gifted to foreign rulers, like the fine pair of brass fishtails in the Museum of Antiquities inscribed 'I L, 1611', which belonged to Louis the Thirteenth of France (see opposite), and the equally fine pair of lemon butts, by the same maker, in the Hermitage, Leningrad. Many were carried abroad by Scottish mercenaries who fought in the Continental wars. Unfortunately, we know little about the makers of these weapons, who usually left only their initials on their work. We can guess with a fair degree of certainty who some of them were. 'I L' was probably James Low, whose name appears in the Dundee hammermen records of the early seventeenth century. Initials on other pistols coincide with the names of gunmakers known to have been active in Dundee at this time.

Heart-butted pistols

In the later seventeenth century, the art of making all-metal pistols spread to the east coast towns of Scotland, like Edzell, Brechin, Inverness and Dundee. From the mid-century onwards all-steel pistols with heart-shaped butts were the most common and, unlike the earlier highly decorated pistols, were often strictly utilitarian. A pricker fitted with a globular head for cleaning out the touch hole is screwed into the base of the butt, as on some lemon-butted pistols (see over). Early heart-butt pistols are fitted with snaphance locks and, indeed, examples of these occur as late as 1686 but, generally speaking, in the later seventeenth century the snaphance was modified in several ways. The steel and pancover, for instance, were combined into one, and a small dog catch was fitted to the lock plate to catch the cock and hold it fast in a 'half-cock' position. As early as the 1660s, the true flintlock, developed on the Continent at the beginning of the century, was adopted. This lock, which was to supersede most others until it in turn was replaced in the early nineteenth century by the percussion lock, was a radical new invention, which worked on an entirely different principle

45

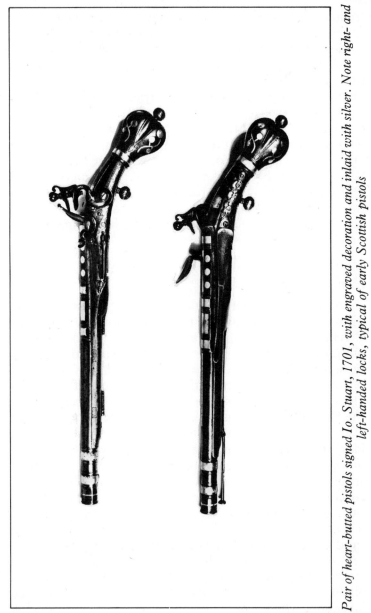

Pair of heart-butted pistols signed Io. Stuart, 1701, with engraved decoration and inlaid with silver. Note right- and left-handed locks, typical of early Scottish pistols

from that of the snaphance and of the more developed 'dog-locks'. Flintlocks have a combined steel and pan-cover and their internal mechanism works vertically instead of horizontally as do the snaphances. Instead of a lug projecting through the lock-plate to keep the cock back ready to fire, the cock is held internally by means of the sear (the moving part acting against the main spring and the tumbler) engaging in a groove cut in the tumbler to which the cock is attached. A second groove in the tumbler ensures that the cock can also be held in a half-cock position for safety.

Production of heart-butted pistols continued until about 1730. Their decoration consists of engraving with inlays of silver or copper wire, and silver bands and plaques in the shape of hearts, flowers, diamonds, and so on. Flower and foliage designs dominate. One of the finest makers of these pistols was an unidentified gunsmith whose initials are 'D H'; an example of his work is in the Royal Scottish Museum. Other finely decorated pistols were made by Io. Stuart and 'G S' (William Smith of Inverness?).

Long guns

Scottish gunmakers of the seventeenth century also showed their ingenuity in making long guns, those intended for sporting purposes often being of high quality in their decoration. There are, unfortunately, fewer than thirty guns from the seventeenth century surviving in a more or less complete state, thirteen of them, including the finest, coming from the private armoury of the lairds of Grant (the Seafield collection), now in the National Museum of Antiquities in Edinburgh.

The earliest complete sporting gun, signed 'R A' (Robert Alison of Dundee?) and dated 1614, is in the Tower of London. Its stock is inlaid in silver with thistle heads and leaves. Another two early examples are both superlative pieces of craftsmanship and are most unusual in being made entirely of brass, probably by James Low of Dundee. One of them, dated 1624, is in the Museum of Antiquities. It is stylistically similar to Low's brass pistols. The butt ends in

Drawing of sporting gun, signed A P, 1635, from the Castle Grant armoury

Drawing of sporting gun, lock signed I T, 1671, barrel I S, 1667, from the Castle Grant armoury. The butt plate is of silver and the barrel has the initials of Ludovic Grant, first Laird of Grant

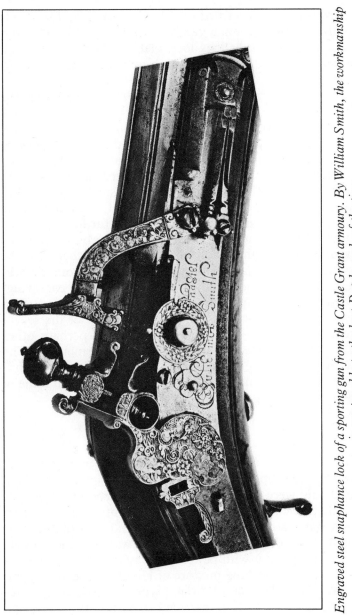

Engraved steel snaphance lock of a sporting gun from the Castle Grant armoury. By William Smith, the workmanship is comparable to the best Dutch work of the time

49

an open-work crown fitted to rods which pull out for adjusting the length. The other gun is in the Tower of London but unfortunately has had its lock plate replaced. It is in all respects similar to the Edinburgh gun, but dates to a few years earlier.

Another early gun, with a wooden stock, *c.* 1635, from the Castle Grant collection, is probably the work of Andrew Philp of Dundee. On its stock are small inlaid silver figures of a man on horseback, a fish and some dogs, in imitation of bone and ivory inlay work of the Continent (see page 48).

All other sporting guns have downward-curving wooden stocks. Like that of the Philp gun their stocks are fluted, a fashion employed on some English guns of the period. In the better quality examples, the stocks are further decorated with foliage and have engraved silver or brass butt plates (see page 48). Although the foliage is Highland in character, the decoration is Lowland, and some of the guns from the Seafield collection show the influence of Dutch engraving. These Highland sporting guns were made by craftsmen working in the north-east in the second half of the seventeenth century. In some cases, barrels and perhaps other parts were imported for mounting by clan armourers. The Laird of Grant's gunsmith was William Smith of Duthil, Inverness-shire, and his name or initials appear on some of the guns (see page 49).

Powderhorns

Powderhorns were so intimately associated with guns that they should be mentioned, especially since some finely decorated ones were produced in seventeenth-century Scotland, mostly in the north-eastern counties. They were made from cows' horns softened in boiling water and then slightly flattened. A wooden plug was put into the wide end and a nozzle made at the point with pewter or brass mounts. The decoration is an interesting mixture of Highland leaf-work, animals and interlace, and Lowland types of decoration. Dates and mottoes were often inscribed (see opposite).

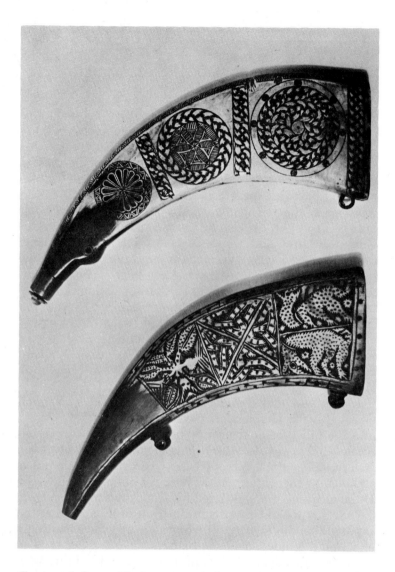

Two powderhorns. The bottom one is decorated with foliage, interlace and animals, and is a good example of seventeenth-century Highland art. The other shows the degeneration of this art into roundels of geometric ornamentation

51

The Weapons of the Clansmen

THE old method of fighting with broadsword and targe survived among the Highlanders into the eighteenth century with notable successes, particularly in the Jacobite uprising of 1745, when an army of clansmen defeated the massed infantry of the British Army in two pitched battles at Preston-pans and Falkirk. Apart from the sword and targe, the main weapons of the Highlanders were pistols, guns, dirks and knives. In a fight, the charge was the most important tactic. Guns were fired and jettisoned before reaching the enemy lines. The targes served to catch the opposing bayonets while the Highlanders' swords wreaked havoc. Pistols and dirks—the latter being held in the left hand along with the targe—were used as a second line of defence. Speed was essential, and for this reason the Highlanders were lightly clad and armed. An eye-witness account of the Battle of Killiecrankie in 1689 describes how Viscount Dundee's Highlanders attacked barefoot, wearing only shirts and little Highland doublets.

It was said that if the enemy stood firm at the initial onslaught, the Highlanders never failed to run away again into the hills, faster than they had come. This was by no means always the case, the Highlanders soon perfecting the technique of taking the opposing bayonets on their targes and flicking them aside. At the Battle of Culloden in 1746 the Duke of Cumberland ordered his troops not to thrust their bayonets at the enemy straight in front of them, but at the exposed flank to their right. This tactic may have had some effect on the outcome of the battle.

The Highlanders' method of hand-to-hand fighting with targe and broadsword was entirely new to the government troops who opposed them. There is an amusing account of an incident which occurred at Killiecrankie during combat between an English soldier and a Highlander. The former was well versed in the use of the backsword, but all his blows fell on his foe's targe, while the Highlander set about the Englishman with his broadsword, cutting him in two or three places. The Englishman, more enraged than injured, cried out to him: "You dog, come out from behind the door and fight like a man!" Fortunately for the Englishman, he was rescued by his friends who also captured the Highlander.

Targes

Although such weapons as basket-hilted swords, dirks and pistols are typical of the arms used by the Highlanders, many of them were produced in the Lowlands. This is not the case with the targes, which were manufactured and used almost solely in the Highland region in the seventeenth and eighteenth centuries. Targes are circular shields consisting of two thin layers of either oak or fir, the grain of one set across the other, and the whole covered in cowhide. They are generally about twenty inches in diameter. Their main characteristic is the rich decoration consisting of brass studs, thin plates of brass and intricate tooled designs in the leather. They usually have a central metal boss, often with a long projecting metal spike. The inside surface is covered with deer- or goat-skin and has a handgrip and a loop for the arm, as well as straps so that it could be carried on the back when not in use.

Targes are the descendants of the circular shields, or targets, used in the fifteenth and sixteenth centuries by men fighting on foot. In an Act of Parliament of 1456, men unable to shoot with a bow were ordered to arm themselves with an axe and a targe constructed either of leather or of fine board, with two bands on the back. Sometimes the targe was reinforced with horn, or made of steel, proof against bullets. The earliest Highland targe that we can date is the one in the Hunterian Museum, Glasgow. The brass central plate bears the date 1623. Most surviving targes, however, belong to the last quarter of the seventeenth and the first half of the eighteenth centuries.

It is possible to divide targes into two main groups, on the basis of their decoration. The first group has designs arranged concentrically round the central boss, the areas of decoration usually defined by rows of nails (see opposite). There are three main sub-groups: first, those with the bands divided into segments by lines radiating from the central boss; second, those in which a star pattern is dominant; and third, those with a series of semi-circular panels around the perimeter.

The second, and numerically the smaller, group consists of targes in which the central boss is surrounded by roundels or lozenges, delineated by rows of studs as in the first group, each containing their own boss (see opposite). To this group belongs the targe in the Hunterian Museum and also the very fine targe in the Museum of Antiquities, said to have been carried by the Marquess of Huntly at the Battle of Sheriffmuir in 1715. It is richly decorated with a silver boss and silver nails.

These different groups of targes may be the result of varying workshop traditions. A targe from St Martin's, Perthshire, dated 1715, now in the Museum of Antiquities, and one from Dunollie Castle may have come from the same workshop, and there is a group of targes which belonged to the Earls of Seafield which are probably the work of one man.

The decoration of the leather was achieved by a combination of embossing and indenting with a blunt tool. The designs are typical of Highland art and consist of interlace, foliage and animals arranged in the partitions formed by the studs. Interlace and foliage are most commonly used, and there is a surprising lack of heraldic motifs. Even when they occur, as in the fine two-headed eagle on a targe from Skye (see opposite), we cannot be sure that the eagle was intended to be recognised as the badge of a particular family. Decoration also takes the form of brass plates, plain or pierced with hearts, circles, and so on, and sometimes with red cloth

54

Targe from St Martin's, Perthshire, engraved with the date 1715 on its silver boss

A targe of type two, with decoration composed of roundels and lozenges with silver studs and boss. Said to have been carried by the Marquess of Huntly at the Battle of Sheriffmuir, 1715

Targe with concentric panels of decoration arranged round a double-headed eagle, late seventeenth century

showing through from beneath (said by some to be from the red coats of government troops). The brass bosses are often lightly engraved.

The dating of targes is difficult, for very few have dates on them. Generally speaking, targes from the late seventeenth and early eighteenth centuries have small nails and intricate designs, while many later targes have large areas covered with plates of metal. Targes were at their best at the end of the seventeenth and beginning of the eighteenth centuries; thereafter the quality of workmanship, in common with that of other objects of Highland manufacture, declined. Prince Charles's army in 1745 was short of targes and many had to be specially made in Perth and Edinburgh, though these were of no artistic merit, we can be sure. Targes failed to survive the '45 as a piece of military equipment and many of those that have come down to us owe their preservation to the fact that they made convenient lids for barrels and churns. Boswell noted this while touring with Dr Johnson in the Highlands in 1773, and targes so used were found at Dun-ollie Castle.

Dirks

Dirks are a late survival in the Highland region of the ballock knives common in medieval times. The term 'dirk' was recorded as early as 1557, when one was drawn in a brawl at Inverness. They may not, at this early stage, have been exclusively Highland weapons, for there was a dirk-maker working in Edinburgh in the late sixteenth century, and others in Perth. These early 'dirks' are possibly what we would now recognise as ballock knives. The earliest surviving weapons are as recent as the late seventeenth century.

Dirks are long-bladed daggers meant essentially for hand-to-hand fighting. They were held in the left hand, point down, and used for stabbing. The blades are 'backed', that is, wedge-shaped in cross-section, and taper to a sharp point. Sometimes a plate of brass is set into the back edge and

A group of early dirks. The one on the far left dates to the early eighteenth century and has a horn grip; its blade is a cut-down sword blade. The one on the far right dates to the second half of the seventeenth century and is similar in form to the earlier ballock knives

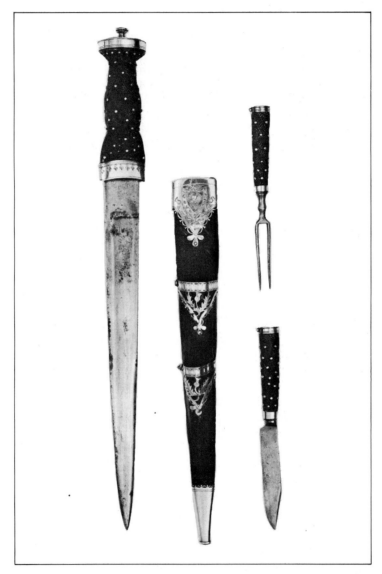

Dirk with baluster-shaped hilt and silver fittings, and knife and fork which fit into pockets in the front of the scabbard. It has Edinburgh hallmarks for 1796-7

engraved. In many early examples the blades are Scottish made, but in the mid-eighteenth century there was a tendency to use cut-down sword blades. The hilts are usually of hardwood, and short in length. Between the blade and the grip, they swell into haunches and the pommel broadens into a disc mounted with a brass or silver plate. There are, however, some dirks with brass hilts, and others of horn and bone. Dirks were carried in leather sheaths attached to the belt. In a little pocket attached to the front of the sheath a small knife was carried and later examples were equipped with knives and forks.

Some early dirks have small, rounded haunches and a marked curve to the bottom of the hilt—two features noticeable also in earlier daggers. A particularly fine example is a dirk of the second half of the seventeenth century in the Museum of Antiquities. Round the grip it has two narrow bands of interlace decoration. In contrast most late seventeenth- and early eighteenth-century dirks have carved interlace patterns over the entire hilt, the bottom edge of the pommel being fluted. The haunches also tend to be more straight-sided. To protect the weak projecting parts, the metal plate on the pommel was gradually extended down to cover the sides as well, and a metal shoe was fitted to the bottom of the hilt, sometimes with straps running up the outer edges of the haunches. By the mid-eighteenth century many dirks were reinforced like this, and metal mounts were fitted to the scabbards.

Dirks continued in popularity after the '45—and indeed are still made and worn to this day—but in the second half of the eighteenth century the design generally degenerated. The proportions were altered and the interlace designs became clumsy or changed into simple basket-work patterns. Metal studs were often interspersed in the interlace, whereas previously little wooden studs had been carved from the solid hilt. By the end of the eighteenth century the grips had tended to acquire a shape rather like a stubby baluster. In the following century this outline was to change into the familiar thistle shape. Many of these later dirks are richly ornamented with silver mounts and engraving, and the pommels mounted with cut stones—'Cairngorms' of a smoky yellow colour are the most common. Some were worn by army officers and hence have battle honours on their blades. The fashion for setting dirks with stones came in about 1800. The stones are often cocked frontwise to show them off to advantage.

Skene dhus

Skene dhu means in Gaelic a black (hilted) knife, but nowadays they are thought of as the small ornamental knives worn in the stockings with Highland dress. There is no evidence of this fashion before the late eighteenth century. Highlanders, at an earlier date, are said to have carried knives concealed in their sleeve near the armpit. Some knives with interlace carved on their hilts have survived.

Later basket-hilted swords

Early in the eighteenth century many basket hilts assumed a form which is still in use today for the dress swords of some army officers. The infilling panels between the vertical bars of the hilt are rectangular and pierced with circles, diamonds, clubs and other shapes. The remnant of the rear quillon is extended and curled upwards in a broad loop, apparently as a precaution against cuts to the wrist. Such swords were carried by the Highlanders—and by their opponents—in the Jacobite uprisings of the eighteenth century. The finest hilts were made by craftsmen working in Glasgow and Stirling, though undoubtedly many were made in other burghs as well. We know the makers of some of these by the initials, or complete names, they put on the hilts, usually on the underside.

In Glasgow, basket hilts of fine quality and traditional pattern were made by John Simpson, father and son, and

Thomas Gemmil, among others. A hilt signed 'I S' on the base of the knuckle bar on a sword said to have belonged to the Marquis of Montrose, now in the Glasgow Museum, is possibly the work of John Simpson senior, who was admitted a freeman of the Incorporation of Hammermen of Glasgow in 1683 and died in 1718. Other swords signed 'I S' over 'G', for Glasgow, are apparently the work of his son, who was admitted a freeman to the Incorporation in 1711 and died in 1749 (see over).

Many of the swords produced by the Stirling swordsmiths are similar to those made in Glasgow. One John Allan was booked as a journeyman to the elder John Simpson in Glasgow in 1702, and it is thought that he is the same John Allan, 'sword slipper in Doune', who was admitted a burgess of Stirling in 1714. Not only does his work show similarity to that of the Simpsons in Glasgow, but Allan decorated some of his finest hilts with inlaid patterns in silver and copper using a technique and designs similar to those developed by the gunsmiths in Doune, whose work is described below. John's son Walter was made a burgess of Stirling in 1732, and his brother John, who also worked as a swordsmith, was made a burgess in 1741. Both appear as debtors in the will of the younger John Simpson of Glasgow, suggesting contacts were maintained. Both Walter and John Allan junior made fine hilts in the style used by their father, sometimes inlaid with metal, but they also, especially Walter, produced variations on the standard theme with more intricate open-work designs with thistles, hearts, lozenges and wavy bars (see page 63). Walter even had all-silver hilts made to his own designs by Colin Mitchell, goldsmith in Canongate.

The finest basket hilts were those produced by the Stirling swordsmiths in the mid-eighteenth century. Thereafter, basket hilts declined in quality, largely because swords of this type were no longer used or worn by civilians, who had taken to wearing small swords, descendants of the earlier rapiers, usually with a knuckle bow, short, up-turned quillons and shells. These swords were rarely used and were often richly decorated. It is evident that many of the makers

Basket-hilted broadsword. The hilt is signed by John Simpson no. 2 of Glasgow, c. 1730-50

Basket-hilted back-sword. The hilt is signed by Walter Allan of Stirling, c. 1735-60

of basket hilts must have turned their attention to these as well as to hangers.

Doune pistols

Doune, a small burgh a few miles from Stirling, situated on the edge of the Highland line, was to become renowned in the eighteenth century as a centre for the manufacture of fine pistols. Owing to its position, it attracted trade from the Highland region. Cattle fairs were held there annually, and so it is not surprising that gun-making flourished. Because the main market for pistols was undoubtedly among the Highland lairds and tacksmen, Doune pistols came to be called Highland pistols. It is important to note, however, that the Doune gunsmiths were working entirely in a Lowland tradition of craftsmanship, and not even the decoration on the pistols shows any clear trace of Highland influence.

The earliest surviving Doune pistol—on show in the Museum of Art and History in Neuchâtel, Switzerland—is dated 1678 and signed by Thomas Caddell. According to the *First Statistical Account* of 1798, a certain Thomas Caddell came from nearby Muthill and settled in Doune in 1646, setting up in business as a gunsmith; but there is no clear evidence that he made pistols. In fact, Caddell described himself only as a smith. He died in 1660, leaving a son, also called Thomas, who may have been the maker of the Neuchâtel pistol. From then we can trace a remarkable succession of gunsmiths, fathers and sons, all called Thomas Caddell and working in the burgh of Doune—four in all, and a Robert Caddell, gunsmith, as well. The Caddells, it would seem, were operating a successful business and the will of the second Thomas Caddell, gunsmith, suggests that the family was by no means poor.

It was not the only family in Doune involved in the gun-making business. From the early eighteenth century onwards we have pistols signed by several other makers, some of whom may have received their training as apprentices in the Caddell workshop, or at least at the hands of the first of Thomas Caddell's pupils. John Campbell, for example, working in the first quarter of the century, was followed in the mid-century by an Alexander Campbell and another John, probably Alexander's son. In the second half of the century, pistols were also made in Doune by John Christie and John Murdoch.

Doune pistols are easily recognisable by their shape and decoration. They are all made entirely of metal, usually steel, and most have a scroll (or ramshorn) butt (see over). The earliest scroll-butted pistols date to the second half of the seventeenth century and may be derived from the fishtail butts of the first quarter of that century. Between the scrolls of the butt is screwed a pricker (for cleaning out the touch hole) with a globular head, in the same form as the trigger. The pistols are richly decorated all over with engraved flowers and scroll-work, and are often inlaid with silver wire, plaques and panels. The earlier pistols are usually longer and less curved than the later ones, and the dominant forms of inlay are plaques and bands. Many pistols made before the Jacobite uprising of 1745 have star-shaped designs on the sides of their grips. From about 1740 onwards oval silver panels to take the owner's name or crest became more common. Typically, the cocks have an ornamental lug decorated as a rose, and the barrels are fluted at the breech, with flared and faceted muzzles. The ramrods are decorated with beading.

The peculiar design of the locks is one of the main characteristics of the group. Externally, they look like true flintlocks, with a combined pan-cover and steel for the flint to strike against, but internally they work in an entirely different fashion. The mechanism of a true flintlock moves vertically, whereas that of Doune pistols moves horizontally, as do the earlier snaphance locks. To retain the cock in a half-cock position, a short lug projects through the lock plate in front of the cock. This feature immediately distinguishes a Doune lock from a real flintlock. The earliest known pistol with this type of lock was made by Thomas Caddell in 1678.

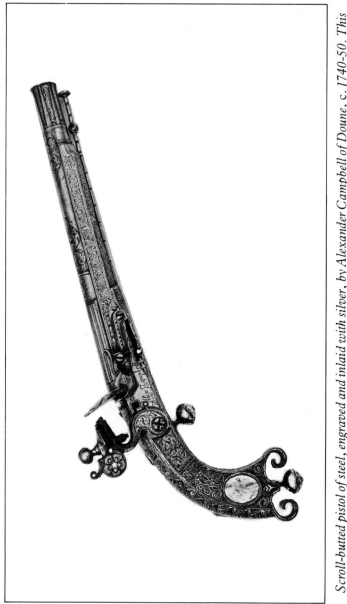

Scroll-butted pistol of steel, engraved and inlaid with silver, by Alexander Campbell of Doune, c. 1740-50. This is an exceptionally fine example of a Doune pistol

As an extra safety measure its cock is fitted with a small catch to hold it in the half-cock position. Perhaps the credit for designing this type of lock ought to go to Thomas, the first of the Caddell pistol-makers, who simply altered the snaphance lock to give it the appearance of the flintlocks current throughout most of Europe from the late seventeenth century onwards. But it is remarkable that Doune locks survived right up to the beginning of the nineteenth century.

The failure of the '45 uprising and the consequent prohibition of arms in the Highlands undoubtedly had an adverse effect on the gun-making industry. Since the Doune gun-makers' business was mostly with the Highland region, they now had to look elsewhere for markets. These they found in the Lowlands and south of the Border, and among the officers and men of the Highland regiments in the British Army, some of whom had been issued with 'Scottish pistols'. These would mostly have been the crude scroll-butt pistols, mass-produced in England and signed by Bissell, or kidney-butted ones bearing the stamp of John Waters. Many officers probably preferred to buy the much superior products of Doune.

Largely owing to the falling off of business in Doune, some of the gunsmiths moved to other towns. Christies established themselves in Stirling and Perth, and Thomas Murdoch moved to Leith in the 1770s. Their connections with Doune are not altogether clear, but their surnames and the style of their work leave little doubt that Doune was their origin. Even before the Jacobite disaster gunsmiths working in the style of Doune had established themselves in other places, notably Daniel Walker in Dumbarton and Hector McNeill in Mull. The latter is an exception, for he was the only 'Doune' pistol-maker known to have worked in the Highland region. Other gunsmiths in the east coast towns were influenced to varying extents by the Doune pistols, some adopting the shape, the lock and the elements of decoration for their own work.

A new type of pistol was developed by the Doune gunsmiths immediately after the '45—pistols with lobe-shaped butts either in steel or in brass. They were thus comparable in shape to the wooden-butted pistols being made in many Lowland towns at this time, and must have been meant as a concession to Lowland taste. Not many of these have survived, and it seems that scroll butts remained the more popular, but Thomas Murdoch of Leith made several of brass, nicely engraved all over with debased acanthus leaf (see opposite).

By the end of the eighteenth century the making of Doune pistols had all but died out. John Murdoch was probably the last gunsmith working in Doune itself, and he is thought to have died in 1812. Thomas Murdoch of Leith died in 1791. Ironically, the death of the last true Doune gunsmiths coincided with an awakening of interest in their work. Already in the 1780s and '90s both had been at least partly responsible for making presentation sets of pistols of the traditional scroll-butt shape, with additional decoration of plaques and gilding, presumably worked by a London or Edinburgh jeweller. These were prestige pieces destined for a select clientele, but soon several gunsmiths in Edinburgh, Glasgow, Aberdeen, and even south of the Border, were turning out scroll-butt pistols for wearing with the newly fashionable Highland dress. These are often contemptuously referred to as costume pistols, and it is in fact the case that most are lacking in the fine proportions and decoration of the Doune pistols. Entirely new decorative motifs, like trophies of arms, were often used. But by the mid-nineteenth century this production had tailed off as well.

Basket-hilted swords, dirks and all-metal pistols continued to be made during the nineteenth century, and indeed edged weapons and targes are still made to this day. But after Culloden—the last battle fought in the British Isles—the great Scottish traditions of arms-making waned. Weapons came to be regarded chiefly as decorative objects, and inevitably the quality of design and workmanship in most cases declined. Fine sporting guns continued to be made in Scotland, especially in Edinburgh, but they were English in design and not of the earlier tradition.

Lobe-butted pistol of steel by Thomas Murdoch of Leith, c. 1770-90

69

By the end of the eighteenth century, arms for the private individual were largely things of the past. The wars of the nineteenth and twentieth centuries were to call for the production of weapons on such a scale and of such inventiveness as were hitherto undreamt of.

Advice on Weapons

MUSEUM curators will give advice on weapons in their own collections and also on those brought in for them to see. The National Museum of Antiquities in Edinburgh keeps records of Scottish weapons, and is always eager to study further examples. Often weapons have been repaired in various ways, swords re-hilted or new parts fitted to a gun lock, and it takes an experienced eye to note such alterations. More and more reproductions of old weapons are being made, and the unwary can easily confuse them with authentic weapons.

A problem with many weapons is how to restore them and keep them in good condition, free from rust and dirt. Decoration can often be lost by over-vigorous cleaning and the appearance of the weapon spoiled. It is therefore advisable to seek professional guidance before attempting restoration work.

Museums do not value objects. Valuations must be obtained from auctioneers or antique dealers. Good-quality Scottish weapons are much sought after, and examples commanding high prices regularly pass through the London sale-rooms of Christie's and Sotheby's. In 1977, for example, a wooden-stocked fishtail pistol dated 1618 fetched £11,000; an eighteenth-century basket-hilted broadsword £460; a late-eighteenth-century lobe-butted Doune pistol £2,000; and a silver-mounted regimental dirk of *c.* 1875, £350. The sale catalogues produced by auctioneers are often a useful source of information.

Where to See Scottish Arms and Armour

THE best collection is undoubtedly that in the National Museum of Antiquities of Scotland in Edinburgh. It is not only a large collection, but also contains representative examples of all the different types of weapons that have survived. Glasgow Art Gallery and Museum also has a very fine collection, as have the Royal Scottish Museum in Edinburgh and Marischal College Museum in Aberdeen. Most local museums have Scottish weapons in varying quantities, and there are still some spectacular collections on display in stately homes, for example at Blair Atholl Castle, Perthshire; Abbotsford, Roxburghshire; and Inveraray Castle, Argyll. Many Scottish weapons are preserved in collections outside Scotland. Both the Tower of London and the Victoria and Albert Museum have interesting collections.

It is as well to remember that many museums cannot put all their weapons on display at one time, and if one wishes to see weapons which are in store, or to make a detailed study of some of them, special provisions can be made for the serious student or inquirer to do so. It is necessary to write to the keepers of the collections well in advance to make an appointment. Most of the larger museums will provide inexpensive photographs of items in their collections.

Some Scottish churches contain effigies of knights in armour, or grave slabs depicting weapons, and it is normally necessary to obtain permission from the minister for access to these. The whereabouts of many of these are listed in the article by R. Brydall (see the Reading List). Some fine examples are in the care of the Inspectorate of Ancient Monuments and are easily accessible, such as the monuments of the Black Douglases in St Bride's, Douglas, Lanarkshire, and the effigies in Seton Collegiate Church, East Lothian. The Inspectorate also cares for many fine

72

West Highland monuments—for example, on Iona and at Kildalton Church in Kintyre. Information about these and many more can be found in the *Guide to Ancient Monuments in Scotland*, obtainable from H.M.S.O. bookshops.

Glossary

Aketon: quilted coat, worn by itself or under armour.

Armet: a type of close-fitting helmet, completely enclosing the head.

Arming jacket: padded jacket, sometimes reinforced with pieces of chain mail, worn as a protection under armour.

Arming sword: a type of one-handed sword.

Back sword: sword with single-edged blade.

Ballock knife: dagger or knife with ballock-shaped hilt.

Basinet: a type of helmet, conical in shape, often fitted with visor and bevor.

Baslar (baselard): a type of dagger worn by civilians.

Besagew: plates attached at the shoulders.

Bevor: chin defence.

Bombard: large cannon, especially for siege work.

Brigandine: jacket reinforced with metal plates riveted together.

Broadsword: sword with double-edged blade.

Buckler: small round shield used when fighting on foot with a sword.

By-knife: knife carried in a pocket in the scabbard of a sword or dagger.

Chausses: leggings of chain mail.

Claymore: two-handed sword used in the Highlands.

Coat armour: cloth garment worn over armour, generally reaching to the hips.

Coif: mail hood, worn under helmet.

Corslet: a breast- and back-plate together.

Cranequin: a rack-and-pinion mechanism for pulling string on crossbow.

Culverin: type of long gun (also name applied to a class of cannon).

Dag: early term for pistol.

Dog lock: gun lock in which the cock is retained in a half-cock position by a small (dog) catch.

Doune lock: type of gun lock superficially similar to a flintlock, but the mechanism operates horizontally.

Dudgeon dagger: a type of dagger worn by civilians.

Fauld: plate defence of the lower torso.

Fencible men: those required to bear arms; militiamen.

Flintlock: type of gun lock in which the mechanism, operating vertically, causes a flint to strike sparks off a steel, thus igniting the charge. The steel and pan-cover are combined.

Gisarme: long-shafted weapon with broad axe-blade.

Gorget: defence for the neck, either of plate or mail.

Greave: plate defence for shin.

Habergeon: mail coat, lighter than a hauberk.

Halberd: long-shafted weapon mounted with a spear-head and axe-blade.

Halflang sword: probably a 'hand-and-a-half' sword, usable with one or two hands.

Halkrig: corslet.

Hammerman: 'one who wields a hammer'—a worker in metal.

Hanger: dagger or small sword (whinger).

Hauberk: coat of chain mail.

Host: the Scottish national army.

Hounskull: type of visor with pointed snout.

Jack: jacket reinforced with metal plates.

Javelin: spear used by light horsemen; also a light throwing spear.

Jedburgh staff: type of long-shafted weapon, possibly with long narrow cutting edge, ending in a point.

Kettle-hat: basin-shaped iron hat, normally with broad brim.
Knapscull: steel bonnet; basin-shaped iron hat.

Langet: tongue of metal, extending up blade from hilt as a strengthening device.
Leather guns: light field pieces bound with leather.
Leith axe: probably a type of long-shafted weapon.
Lochaber axe: probably a long-shafted weapon mounted with a broad cutting blade.

Match-lock: simple type of gun lock on which the charge is ignited by a lighted match.
Morion: metal cap of semi-oval outline with flat rim.
Mortuary hilt: sword hilt decorated with head, said to represent the martyred Charles the First.

Pauldron: shoulder defence.
Pellet bow: bow used for hunting, which fired lead or clay pellets.
Pisane: mail defence for the neck and shoulders or the head and shoulders.
Pommel: knob at end of hilt, which balances blade and secures it to the grip.

Quillons: cross-guard separating hilt from blade.

Rapier: sword with long slender thrusting blade.
Ribbon hilt: type of basket hilt, cut and forged with broad flat strips of metal.

Sallet: type of helmet with round skull, often extending into a point at the back.
Sear: part of gun lock which operates against the mainspring and tumbler.
Serpentine: small cannon.
Skene dhu: small knife worn in the top of the stocking.

Small sword: type of sword worn with civilian clothing, often little more than a decoration.

Snaphance: type of gun lock in which the mechanism operates horizontally, causing a flint to strike sparks off a steel, thus igniting the charge. The steel and pan-cover are unconnected.

Splint: plate defence for arm or leg.

Surcoat: cloth coat worn over armour.

Targe: circular shield used when fighting on foot.

Tassets: plate defences for the upper thighs.

Took: term for a sword with a long, stiff, pointed blade.

Tumbler: part of gun lock that receives thrust of main spring and forces cock forward.

Vambraces: armour for the forearms.

Vamplate: hand-guard on a long-shafted weapon.

Visor: face piece.

Wageour: mercenary.

Wappinschawingis: meetings at which the arms and armour of the fencible men were inspected.

Whinger (hanger): dagger or small sword.

Windlass: mechanism for pulling string on crossbow.

Reading List

SURPRISINGLY little research has been done on Scottish weapons, despite the great fascination that they have held for Scots and foreigners alike; and much that has been written is out of date. Listed below are some of the more recent and accessible books and articles on the subject. By using the references given in these, the interested reader can be put in touch with many other works.

'The Doune Pistol Makers', J. Arthur and D. H. Caldwell (*Guns Review*, Vol. 16, 1976).

Late Medieval Monumental Sculpture in the West Highlands, K. Steer and J. Bannerman (Royal Commission on the Ancient and Historical Monuments of Scotland, 1977). (Contains useful account of early Highland arms and armour and depictions of them on grave slabs.)

'The Monumental Effigies of Scotland from the Thirteenth to the Fifteenth Century', R. Brydall (*Proceedings of the Society of Antiquaries of Scotland*, Vol. 29, 1894-95).

Scottish Arms Makers, C. E. Whitelaw (Arms and Armour Press, 1977). (Also republishes pioneering papers on dirks, basket hilts and dog-lock mechanisms.)

'Scottish Firearms', C Blair (*Bulletin of the American Society of Arms Collections*, Vol. 31, 1975).

'Scottish Pistols', G. Boothroyd (*Journal of the Arms and Armour Society*, Vol. 6, 1969).

Scottish Swords and Dirks, J. Wallace (Arms and Armour Press, 1970).

'Scottish Weapons' (*Scottish Art Review*, Vol. 9, 1963, special number). (Contains articles on targes, armour, basket-hilted swords, dudgeon daggers, heart-butted pistols, etc.)